SOCIAL MEDIA:
Like It or
Leave It

by Rebecca Rowell

Content Consultant
Paul Leonardi
Reece Duca Professor of Technology Management
University of California, Santa Barbara

COMPASS POINT BOOKS
a capstone imprint

Compass Point Books are published by Capstone,
1710 Roe Crest Drive, North Mankato, Minnesota 56003
www.capstonepub.com

Editorial Credits
Melissa York, editor; Becky Daum and Craig Hinton, designers; Maggie Villaume,
production specialist; Catherine Neitge and Ashlee Suker, consulting editor
and designer

Photo Credits
Like It
AP Images: Boris Grdanoski, 11, Sue Ogrocki, 13; Shutterstock Images: Artishock,
cover; Everett Collection, 24, junpinzon, 15, Luba V Nel, 5, Quka, 23, Wave Break
Media, 9; Thinkstock: Anatoliy Babiy, 16, Catherine Yeulet, 19, william87, 21

Leave It
AP Images: *Star Tribune*, Mark Vancleave, 5; Shutterstock Images: Artishock,
cover, Halfpoint, 24, Light Wave Media, 11, Maigi, 7, Syda Productions, 26, Sylvie
Bouchard, 17, tarasov, 28, Wave Break Media, 21; Thinkstock: Monkey Business
Images, 12, 15, Steve Hix/Fuse, 23

Library of Congress Cataloging-in-Publication Data
Social media : like it or leave it / Rebecca Rowell.
pages cm. —(Perspectives flip books: issues)
Includes bibliographical references.
ISBN 978-0-7565-4994-7 (library binding)
ISBN 978-0-7565-5024-0 (paperback)
ISBN 978-0-7565-5047-9 (ebook PDF)
1. Social media. I. Title.
HM1206.R694 2015
302.23'1—dc23   2014026596

Printed in the United States of America in Stevens Point, Wisconsin.
092014   008479WZS15

TABLE OF CONTENTS

Shared Resources

Chapter 1

IMPROVING LIVES

A teenager from Iowa City, Iowa, made headlines using social media to send messages to his classmates at West High School. He did not use hurtful words, as is so common in news reports, nor was he joking around. No, he was taking a stand against hateful behavior.

Jeremiah Anthony had read an article about cyberbullies, and he disapproved of them. "You shouldn't be such a coward you have to hide behind a screen and say bad things to people," he said. He decided to take action by using the technology to do good instead. He created an account on Twitter to send compliments to classmates and even teachers. The microblogging site allows messages up to 140 characters. Names called handles begin with the @ symbol.

Jeremiah and his buddies have tweeted more than 3,000 affirmations via the Twitter handle @WestHighBros. For example, they tweeted to one classmate, "Very creative and wise. You're an outstanding musician, with your guitar and your voice. Keep being lovely and caring of all." And they tweeted to another friend, "Your encouraging personality and generosity toward others makes you very likeable. You're quite the intelligent kid, keep it up."

Social media can connect people in positive ways.

Response to the project has been good, and students and the community have followed Jeremiah's lead by sending positive tweets of their own. Jeremiah's tweet project is only one small example of the many ways people use social media and social networking sites including Twitter to do good.

Social Media Basics

The varied and numerous forms of social media allow users to communicate electronically, create online

Social media and social networking are not the same. But sometimes people use the terms interchangeably. Social networking is connecting with others—it can be online or through real-life, offline communities. Social media are the methods people use to share material online. Users connect with one another in online social networks using social media. Facebook friends, for example, send each other photos and messages.

communities, and share a wide range of material, including ideas, information, messages, photos, and videos. Social media includes blogs, wikis, photo sharing services, and instant messaging. Online reviews, bookmarking, and virtual worlds are also social media.

Social media is all about the user. And that makes it very different from TV, newspapers, and other forms of traditional media. With social media, users create the material. More than that, users can comment on each other's material. Responses can range from a simple thumbs-up or thumbs-down to a rave or rant several paragraphs long. The right-now aspect of social media also makes it different from traditional media. Readers can send a letter to the editor in response to a story printed in a magazine, but it won't be published for weeks, if at all. Social media users can share their thoughts and opinions in real time, with anyone and everyone, posting their feedback with the click of a button as soon as they create it.

With dozens of options, social media seems to have something for everyone. And the possibilities for sharing and connecting continue to grow. Millions and millions of people use social media. Facebook alone has almost 1.3 billion members. With such support and continued growth, social media is here to stay. And as many people would argue, understanding what it offers—good and bad—will help new and experienced users of all ages get the most out of all the wonders social media offers.

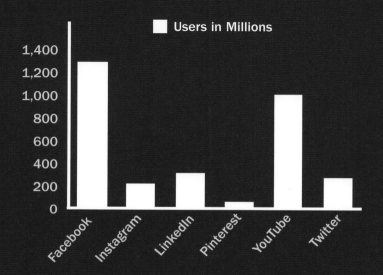

Active Social Media Users, 2014

Users in Millions

1,400	
1,200	
1,000	
800	
600	
400	
200	
0	

Facebook   Instagram   LinkedIn   Pinterest   YouTube   Twitter

Chapter 2

USING SOCIAL MEDIA FOR GOOD

Social media is great for connecting personally and professionally. Users do good deeds with social media, engaging people in ways that teach, make connections, help others, and even fight crime. Or social media can simply make someone's day better, sharing photos or videos that are funny, entertaining, inspiring, or just warm and fuzzy.

Teaching and Connecting

One of social media's positives is its ability to act as a teaching tool. Tutorials cover a variety of topics, such as videos that demonstrate cooking or applying makeup. For example, Rosanna Pansino shares baking

Social media has become an important teaching tool.

ideas via her YouTube channel, Nerdy Nummies. Recipes include Tetris cookies and SpongeBob lemon bars. More than 1 million users subscribe to Nerdy Nummies. They are primarily girls ages 13 to 17. Social media allows Pansino to reach an audience far beyond her friends, family, and local community.

Social media's subject matter also can be profound and affect lives. The National Institute of Mental Health regularly hosts Twitter chats with experts on a variety of topics. Examples include autism, depression, and suicide prevention. Anyone with a Twitter account can participate in the conversation.

The Mayo Clinic hosts chats too. Topics have included migraines, arthritis, and skin cancer. And the world-famous medical center does not limit its sharing of medical knowledge to English. In 2013 Mayo held its first Twitter chat in Spanish, making important medical information available to more social media users.

Organizations use social media to raise awareness and hold fund-raising campaigns. The American Red Cross provides aid when disasters occur in the United States and around the world. The organization has a Facebook page with more than 620,000 "likes." The Red Cross uses its page to share photos and stories of volunteers helping people in need. A post on May 1, 2014, explained, "More than 800 volunteers have stepped up to help those affected by tornadoes and floods." And people respond to such posts. Users commented with words of support such as "Volunteers are AMAZING PEOPLE!!" and "The Red Cross rocks!!"

People Helping People

People use social network sites to reconnect with lost friends and family, ask for advice, buy and sell items, and help people in need directly. Social media users teamed up to help each other in response to the tornadoes that devastated Oklahoma in May 2013. The natural disasters destroyed homes and sent precious items flying. People

Photos of the relief efforts of the Red Cross and other humanitarian organizations worldwide collect positive comments through social media.

many miles away found photographs and personal documents such as letters, valentines, and baseball cards belonging to tornado victims.

Leslie Hagelberg found a photograph near her mailbox in West Tulsa, approximately 90 miles (145 kilometers) from Shawnee, where a tornado had hit. She created a Facebook group to help victims recover their precious mementos, called May 19th 2013 OK Tornado Doc & Picture Recovery. The next day, a tornado hit Moore, Oklahoma, and that spiked interest in the page Hagelberg created. The number of members grew to more than 11,000. Users posted shots of items they had found, hoping the owners would

Crowdfunding

For many people with creative projects, such as developing a book, film, or album, money is often a roadblock to bringing their ideas to life. Aspiring dreamers and entrepreneurs can take to social media for crowdfunding. Through sites such as Kickstarter, users can seek and give donations that support creative projects. Founded in 2009, more than 6 million users have promised $1 billion, mostly through small donations, providing money for approximately 61,000 projects.

see them. Hagelberg's page is one of many designed to help such victims recover personal keepsakes.

Fighting Crime

Many police forces have begun using information collected from social media to fight crime. They also use social media to share information with their communities. For example, Chad Sheehan, a police officer in Sioux City, Iowa, uses Facebook and Twitter to inform users about suspects and to get leads on crimes.

Fighting crime with social media is happening well beyond U.S. borders. In Brazil, Vasco Furtado, a computer science professor at Universidade de Fortaleza, launched

WikiCrimes in 2007 to provide a place where residents can report crimes. If they prefer, users can report anonymously. Authorities can use the information to catch criminals, especially by identifying high-crime areas. WikiCrimes also provides citizens a venue for reaching out for help and for fighting crime.

From prompting an individual smile to sharing information about hobbies, health, and helping, social media has great power for positive action. It might even improve society.

The Oklahoma City Sheriff's Office is one of many law enforcement agencies that uses social media for community outreach.

Chapter 3

MANAGEABLE RISKS

With all its possibilities for creativity, sharing information, and connecting with friends, family, classmates, and more, social media has lots of appeal. But it has cons in addition to its pros. Users can get the most from social media by understanding its risks and knowing how best to deal with them. Many people believe the benefits of social media outweigh these risks, and they argue that savvy people can manage their social media use responsibly.

Use a Critical Eye

"Don't believe everything you read" is a popular saying. It is especially true regarding social media. Because anyone can post anything online, proceed with caution when evaluating content and other users.

Social media has risks, but these risks can be navigated with caution.

Social media content is mostly created by its users, and no gatekeeper or expert makes sure it is accurate.

Approaching material on the Internet with a critical eye is important. Pay attention to sources. Compare them and the content. Consider its location—for example, Wikipedia versus the front page of the *Washington Post*'s website. Wikipedia's content is posted by its users, whereas the reporting in the *Washington Post* is edited and fact-checked by professional journalists. But blogs at the *Washington Post* are less authoritative than news and feature articles. Take note of who posted it—is the poster an expert with official credentials? Thinking critically about online material will help users get the most from the useful and

Consider the source of what you read on the Internet.

entertaining information the Internet has to offer and avoid believing and quoting misinformation.

Oversharing

Social networking sites encourage sharing, but posting some information can be harmful or even dangerous. Providing a cell phone number, e-mail address, school name, or home address allows strangers to easily find a user in real life. Posting a school name or home address does too. Limiting others' access to this information means limiting online predators' access. Being selective about handles and similar names is also important. A sexy or suggestive name might also attract an online predator.

Oversharing can also negatively affect a person's job or college applications. Many colleges and companies check out potential candidates' profiles on social networks. For example, photos on Facebook showing bad behavior might send employers away.

Some things people should keep off their profiles include:

- Any embarrassing information or posts
- Any very personal information or posts
- Photos involving reckless or illegal activities
- Suggestive or sexual photos

It is very difficult to permanently and completely delete posts or photos from the Internet, so it is important people carefully consider what they upload.

Potential Employers

Many employers view job candidates' personal profiles on social media. Employment website CareerBuilder surveyed 2,303 people who work in human resources and who hire employees and learned that 37 percent of them screen prospective employees via social media. These employers use profiles to learn about candidates and to figure out if candidates will be a good fit with the company. The biggest reason employers view profiles is to learn if candidates present themselves professionally. Given this, social media users might want to present themselves in the best possible light—a potential employer could be reading.

Stand Up to Cyberbullies

Bullying through social media, including name-calling, teasing, making threats, and spreading rumors, is called cyberbullying. It takes various forms. Mean messages via e-mail and text are cyberbullying, and so are embarrassing photos and videos. Some cyberbullies spread rumors via e-mail or posts on social networking sites, and some create fake profiles.

Cyberbullying is a serious problem because it is often public, and it may never disappear from the Internet. An embarrassing photo or rumor spread on Twitter can pass through an entire school almost instantly. But users can take steps to stop cyberbullying. If someone receives a message from a cyberbully, he or she should not respond to it or send it to friends. Instead, the recipient should save the message as evidence against the bully and block him or her. The victim and any witnesses can report the bullying to the site where it occurred. If the bullying includes threats or photos that invade privacy, report it to the police. Schools can help too. Let school authorities know about instances of cyberbullying. Working together, users and authorities can help the victim and the person who bullies and create an online social network that is the best it can be.

Reporting cyberbullies can help stop them.

Turn Off Comments

Posting personal thoughts and feelings online can be a healing or creative experience. And receiving positive comments in return can be validating. But comments can also be less than kind, and even hurtful.

An easy way to avoid this possible negative experience is to turn off the comments feature. This is the part of a blogging tool that allows blog readers to post whatever they want. Blogging tools such as WordPress allow various options for enabling or disabling comments.

Guidelines for Good Use

Using a critical eye, saying no to predators, and blocking bullies are good rules for being as safe as possible when using social media. In addition, many websites and organizations post guidelines for best practices in social media use.

Facebook has community standards that outline what is unacceptable on the site. To create a safe environment, Facebook does not allow violence and threats, bullying and harassment, hate speech, or nudity and pornography. To help meet its goals for a safe site, Facebook allows users to report abuse and control what users and content they see.

Many companies and organizations have guidelines for social media use for employees and members too.

The Girl Scouts of America organization has tips to make social networking online healthy and fun, including being yourself, focusing on the positive, and watching out for things that are untrue or fake.

Social media has risks, but many would argue that they are manageable. Knowing what they might face online and understanding the best approaches for addressing potential hazards, users are better able to create fun, healthy social media worlds.

Following basic guidelines keeps social media fun and safe.

NOW AND THE FUTURE

In its relatively brief existence, social media has become a powerful force. Social media use is now the top activity on the Internet. People ages 18 to 34 access YouTube more than any cable television network, and the video sharing site tops 1 billion visitors per month. Social media has created new ways for people, groups, and organizations to express themselves and communicate. And it has connected individuals in many nations and from many cultures.

Facebook's summary of itself describes social media well: "Facebook gives people around the world the power to publish their own stories, see the world through the eyes of many other people, and connect

The variety of social media websites and apps available continues to increase.

and share wherever they go. The conversation that happens on Facebook—and the opinions expressed here—mirror the diversity of the people using Facebook."

Powerful Marketing Tool

Pop superstar Beyoncé tapped the power of social media in December 2013 when she launched a new album. She completely bypassed traditional marketing methods. Usually a record company spends millions of dollars promoting the upcoming release for months and then holds a big release party. Instead, Beyoncé kept the album a secret. Then, on December 12, she posted a short

Beyoncé used the power of social media in new ways to sell her 2013 album.

video on Instagram with a one-word caption: "Surprise!" With 8 million Instagram followers, she had a major audience for her announcement. She relied on the power of social media to spread the word of her new release, *Beyoncé*, complete with 14 songs and 17 music videos. News of her album traveled fast, producing 1.2 million tweets in 12 hours.

The singer shared her reason for promoting the album via social media: "I didn't want to release my music the way I've done it. ... There's so much that gets between the music, the artist, and the fans. I felt like I didn't want anybody to give the message when my record is coming out. I just want this to come out when it's ready and from me to my fans."

Beyoncé's approach was successful. On its first day, U.S. fans bought 365,000 copies of the album. In three days it sold 828,773 copies around the world. She showed her record company, the music industry, and the world how to market successfully using social media.

Traditional Media and Social Media Merge

Social media is changing some traditional media too. Hofstra University surveyed almost 200 directors of television news about social media in 2012. Most directors noted using Facebook, Twitter, or both to connect and interact with users, including getting feedback. Radio stations also use the technology.

Popular television personalities take advantage of social media as well. Television host and comedian Jimmy Fallon is adept at social media, using Facebook, Twitter, and Tumblr. Fallon incorporates Twitter into *The Tonight Show* via skits. And he asks viewers to tweet on a particular topic via a weekly hashtag, such as #MyWeirdFamily and #MyWorstCar. He reads some of the tweets later that week on his late-night program. The show's mascot, a person in a panda suit, has a Twitter-inspired name: Hashtag. Just like businesses and other groups, Fallon uses social media to connect with viewers in numerous ways and in real time. Using social media helps Fallon attract users too, including a demographic that is younger than ever before—some of them teenagers—for the popular and long-standing TV show.

Social Media in Schools

Social media is expanding into other areas as well. Some teachers and schools are taking advantage of it to help students. Elizabeth Delmatoff uses a social media program with her seventh graders in Portland, Oregon. Some of the class's activities include creating collaborative blogs and using social media to discuss news events and complete extra assignments. After a year of the program, grades had improved by more than 50 percent and chronic absenteeism had dropped. Other teachers have incorporated it into the classroom as well. Matt Hardy, a

Cyberbullying Laws

Cyberbullying has become a serious concern for many schools and families. Educators have the authority to deal with bullying that happens on school grounds. But cyberbullying often happens outside of school. So who should be responsible for stopping it?

Several U.S. states have passed or proposed laws to protect victims of cyberbullying. Some laws give schools power to intervene in cyberbullying only when it happens at school or during school-related activities. Other laws say that when cyberbullying interferes with education, schools should take action even if the cyberbullying itself happens outside of school. In states without cyberbullying laws, some schools still take action no matter when or where cyberbullying happens. Others feel they have no right to intervene outside of school, and that responsibility should fall to parents or police.

Minnesota teacher, uses blogs with his third and fourth graders as a tool to encourage writing.

Delmatoff explains why embracing the technology is important: "Don't fight a losing battle. We're going to get there anyway, so it's better to be on the cutting edge, and be moving with the kids, rather than moving against them. ... Should they be texting their friends during a lecture? Of course not. They shouldn't be playing cards in a lecture, they shouldn't be taking a nap during a lecture. But should they learn how to use media for good? Absolutely."

Changing Demographics

Facebook turned 10 years old in February 2014. As the social networking leader reached the milestone, teens were heading to other social networking sites to connect. Popular choices included Instagram and Snapchat for sharing images and Ask.fm, Pheed, and Twitter for networking. In fact, a 2013 survey by investment bank Piper Jaffray found that Facebook's popularity with teens had dropped so much during the preceding year that more teens picked Twitter as their top social networking site.

For today's youth, social media is the norm, whether it involves consulting Wikipedia, watching funny cat videos on YouTube, or tweeting about the events of the day. The online world continues to grow and change, and so does its audience. The online newspaper *Huffington Post* reported in November 2013 that the fastest growing social media demographic on Twitter is users ages 55 to 64, which have increased by 79 percent since 2012. And the 45-to-54 age group was the fastest growing on Facebook and Google+. While they are not digital natives, members of these groups are making social media their norm. This means that companies and organizations that rely increasingly on social media to connect with customers will need to keep this shift in mind.

Social media is connecting family, friends, and strangers. It is building brands and strengthening customer service. It is teaching, helping, and entertaining. It is changing marketing, traditional media, and education. Social media is vast and its possibilities many. It has risks, but many argue that users can easily understand and navigate them. Social media is changing lives for the better, and it is here to stay. Explore and enjoy!

Do Not Believe All the Negative News

Common Sense Media, which advocates for children, surveyed more than 1,000 teens ages 13 to 17 about social media. "On the whole, teens said that they feel that social media has a more positive than negative impact on their social and emotional lives," said Shira Lee Katz, the nonprofit's digital media director. "They believe that social media helps their friendships, makes them feel more outgoing, and gives them confidence." As for the negative side of social media often reported by the media, she said, "For every heartbreaking case of cyberbullying, there are many stories of teens using social media for good."

WHAT DO YOU THINK?

- How do you use social media? Do you think you should use it more or less? How could you use it differently? Why?

- What do you think about parents being involved in their kids' social media use? Do you think it is a good idea? Why or why not?

- What would you do to limit or end cyberbullying?

- If you have never supported an organization such as the Red Cross, do you think you would do so via social media? Explain.

- Is there something you would like to be able to do with social media that is not possible now? In other words, what would you like people to be able to do with social media in the future?

INDEX

INTERNET SITES

Use FactHound to find Internet sites related to this book. All of the sites on FactHound have been researched by our staff.

Here's all you do:
Visit *www.facthound.com*
Type in this code: 9780756549947

GLOSSARY

avatar—an online representation of a user, including a small picture or an animated character in a game

banality—something that is everyday, commonplace, or boring

block—when one user keeps another user from reaching him or her

crowdfunding—asking many people, especially via social media, to give money for a project

defamation—saying something untrue about someone to make that person look bad to others

hashtag—a word or phrase following a # symbol that categorizes the text sent with it, such as a tweet

millennial—a person born in the 1980s or 1990s

podcast—an audio or video file, such as of a talk or music program, that is available online

pornography—printed or visual material that shows nudity or sex to sexually arouse the viewer

upload—to transfer a file from a computer or similar device to the Internet

PROS AND CONS: LIKE IT

Pros

Social media is a great way to connect with others for educational and social purposes.

Information, opinions, and feedback are shared much more quickly than via traditional media.

People use social media to help each other and causes they support.

The risks of social media are manageable.

Cons

Social media opens users to many risks, including cyberbullying, online predators, and crime and identity theft.

Once something has been posted, it is nearly impossible to remove it from the Internet.

Embarrassing social media use can lead to lost job or college opportunities.

PROS AND CONS: LEAVE IT

Pros

Limiting or halting social media use protects users from risks of cyberbullying, online predators, and online crime and identity theft.

Limiting social media use leaves people with more time to enjoy the real world and the outdoors.

People who don't use social media can't post embarrassing photos or information about themselves.

Cons

Social media use is very prevalent, and avoiding it means a person isn't participating in the conversation.

Social media avoiders can't build a positive presence on social media.

Social media offers many opportunities to learn, teach, and interact that avoiders will miss.

CRITICAL THINKING USING THE COMMON CORE

1. This book presents reasons for and against participating in social media. Pick an example from each perspective that you think does a good job of supporting the argument and explain why you think it is a strong example. (Key Ideas and Details)

2. Compare the pros and cons. Weighing the evidence, which is stronger? Is there an additional point that could help make the argument stronger? Explain your answer. (Integration of Knowledge and Ideas)

3. How has this book affected your thoughts or opinions about social media? (Key Ideas and Details)

BOOKS IN THIS SERIES

Animal Testing: Lifesaving Research vs. Animal Welfare

Punishing Bullies: Zero Tolerance vs. Working Together

School Lunches: Healthy Choices vs. Crowd Pleasers

Social Media: Like It or Leave It

SELECT BIBLIOGRAPHY

"Cyberbullying." StopBullying.gov. U.S. Department of Health and Human Services. 5 May 2014. http://www.stopbullying.gov/cyberbullying/

Konnikova, Maria. "How Facebook Makes Us Unhappy." NewYorker.com. 10 Sept. 2013. 5 May 2014. http://www.newyorker.com/tech/elements/how-facebook-makes-us-unhappy

Pulido, Mary L. "Social Media Gone Awry: Tips for Teens to Stay Safe." HuffingtonPost.com. 22 March 2013. 5 May 2014. http://www.huffingtonpost.com/mary-l-pulido-phd/social-media-gone-awry-ti_b_2923603.html

Smith, Jacquelyn. "How Social Media Can Help (or Hurt) You in Your Job Search." Forbes.com.16 April 2013. 5 May 2014. http://www.forbes.com/sites/jacquelynsmith/2013/04/16/how-social-media-can-help-or-hurt-your-job-search/

Wallace, Kelly. "The Upside of Selfies: Social Media Isn't All Bad for Kids." CNN.com. 22 Nov. 2013. 5 May 2014. http://edition.cnn.com/2013/11/21/living/social-media-positives-teens-parents/

Waters, John K. The Everything Guide to Social Media: All You Need to Know About Participating in Today's Most Popular Online Communities. Avon, Mass.: Adams Media, 2010.

FURTHER READING

Bennett, Ruth. Tips for Good Social Networking. New York: Gareth Stevens Publishing, 2014.

Greve, Meg. Social Media and the Internet. Vero Beach, Fla.: Rourke Educational Media, 2013.

Minton, Eric. Online Predators and Privacy. New York: PowerKids Press, 2014.

Raatma, Lucia. Cyberbullying. Danbury, Conn.: Children's Press, 2013.

A Perspectives Flip Book

SOCIAL MEDIA:
Like It or
Leave It

by Rebecca Rowell

Content Consultant
Paul Leonardi
Reece Duca Professor of Technology Management
University of California, Santa Barbara

COMPASS POINT BOOKS
a capstone imprint

ABOUT THE AUTHOR

Rebecca Rowell has authored and edited books for young readers on a variety of topics. One of her favorite parts of writing is doing research and learning about all kinds of subjects. Rowell has a master's degree in publishing and writing from Emerson College. She currently lives in Minneapolis, Minnesota.

SOURCE NOTES

Like It

Page 4, line 8: Eun Kyung Kim. "Teen Uses Tweets to Compliment His Classmates." Today.com. 8 Jan. 2013. 18 April 2014. http://www.today.com/news/teen-uses-tweets-compliment-his-classmates-1B7882246

Page 5, line 6: Ibid.

Page 10, line 13: "American Red Cross." Facebook.com. 1 May 2014. 2 May 2014. https://www.facebook.com/photo.php?fbid=10152366516670071&set=pb.24472055070.-2207520000.1403185291.&type=3&theater

Page 22, line 11: "Facebook Community Standards." Facebook.com. 2014. 2 May 2014. https://www.facebook.com/communitystandards

Page 24, line 9: Jackie Huba. "Beyoncé Uses Only Word of Mouth to Market Surprise New Album." *Forbes*. 17 Dec. 2013. 4 May 2014. http://www.forbes.com/sites/jackiehuba/2013/12/17/beyonce-uses-only-word-of-mouth-to-market-surprise-new-album/

Page 27, line 4: Sarah Kessler. "The Case for Social Media in Schools." Mashable.com. 29 Sept. 2010. 4 May 2014. http://mashable.com/2010/09/29/social-media-in-school/

Page 28, sidebar, line 5: Kelly Wallace. "The Upside of Selfies: Social Media Isn't All Bad for Kids." CNN.com. 22 Nov. 2013. 5 May 2014. http://edition.cnn.com/2013/11/21/living/social-media-positives-teens-parents/

Leave It

Page 4, line 1: Paul Levy. "Tweet Furor: Rogers Student Says He's Sorry, Changes Schools." *Star Tribune*. 24 Feb. 2014. 5 May 2014. http://www.startribune.com/local/west/246805341.html

Page 4, line 13: Ibid.

Page 6, sidebar, line 4: Taryn Ryder. "Sarah Jessica Parker and Other Stars Fight Back Against Twitter Haters." Yahoo.com. 1 May 2014. 5 May 2014. https://celebrity.yahoo.com/blogs/yahoo-celebrity/-sarah-jessica-parker-explains-twitter-feud-over-her-twins-211900688.html

Page 14, sidebar, line 3: Maria Konnikova. "How Facebook Makes Us Unhappy." NewYorker.com. 10 Sept. 2013. 5 May 2014. http://www.newyorker.com/tech/elements/how-facebook-makes-us-unhappy

Page 14, line 8: Martin Robbins. "Facebook Will Destroy Your Children's Brains." *Guardian*. 1 Aug. 2011. 25 July 2014. http://www.theguardian.com/science/the-lay-scientist/2011/aug/01/1

Page 25, sidebar, line 4: "About." National Day of Unplugging. 2013. 6 May 2014. http://nationaldayofunplugging.com/about-us/

Page 26, line 1: Denis Campbell. "Children Growing Weaker As Computers Replace Outdoor Activity." *Guardian*. 21 May 2011. 6 May 2014. http://www.theguardian.com/society/2011/may/21/children-weaker-computers-replace-activity

Page 26, line 7: Ibid.

TABLE OF CONTENTS

LIVES CHANGED

"I never meant to hurt anybody," Reid Sagehorn explained. But he had hurt people, including himself.

Like a lot of teens, the 17-year-old used social media for fun. A senior honor student at Rogers High School in Minnesota, Reid's playful use of the technology included a two-word tweet in January 2014 confirming he had kissed a teacher. Someone had asked on Ask.fm, an ask-and-answer social networking site, if Reid had "made out" with the young woman. The captain of the football and basketball teams responded sarcastically via his Twitter account, "Actually, yes." He said of his brief message, "I thought everybody would take it as a joke." Reid was wrong.

School authorities took his tweet very seriously because teachers and students are not supposed to

Reid Sagehorn (right, with his parents) had to change high schools over something he tweeted. He later sued the school.

interact romantically. If Reid's words were true, the teacher's career could be over. The principal suspended Reid for seven weeks. Reid began having anxiety attacks after his suspension began. The city police chief threatened felony charges for defamation.

Reid changed schools. Students and parents protested. The story went viral. The teen's two-word tweet changed his life and the community. What might have been nothing more than a tasteless but private joke had he been talking to his friends in person, became instead a highly public incident. He hurt his teacher and risked her reputation and career. He had to change schools in the last year of high school. And he can never undo the tweet.

Reid's story represents only one of the possible risks of participating in social media. Inappropriate material, such as a sexually suggestive photo, might hurt a user's reputation. A potential employer might decide not to hire a job candidate based on that material. Illegal activities documented on social media can lead to real-life legal trouble.

Social media can hurt in less tangible ways too. Not all social media users are kind. Some purposely seek to annoy or hurt others. Some leave nasty comments on news articles and blog posts, while others are cyberbullies. In rare and extreme cases, people who were bullied have committed suicide.

Constantly Connected

Social media encompasses the many ways people can communicate electronically. Social media has many formats. Photo-sharing services, instant messaging, and blogs are just a few. Some content posted through these

Jennifer Lawrence Says No

Hunger Games star Jennifer Lawrence avoids social networking sites. She explained why: "It's kind of become funny to make fun of each other, and I also don't like other women slaughtering women. And all of us are just being so mean. We're so responsible for this younger generation, and media, it's what kids are watching. It's teaching people how to talk to each other and relate to each other. I don't like it. Why can't we just be nice? It's like we grow up and then get right back into high school."

The many types of social media websites and apps allow people to share all kinds of information.

formats is educational, intended to inform those who read or view it. For example, people create pages on Wikipedia and post video tutorials on YouTube. Other material is personal and reveals some aspect of the person who provided it, such as his or her birthday, an opinion, or a creative endeavor. Examples include Facebook profiles, reviews on Yelp, and blog posts on WordPress. Still other material is professional, related to the user's job. Résumés on LinkedIn are an example.

Social media enables users to share information with users near and far. People can also stay connected with friends and family or form new connections. Businesses

and organizations also use it. Despite all it has to offer, though, social media has a dark side. Its many avenues for communication create possibilities for bad behavior. In addition to bullies, predators and other abusive people inhabit social media. Their online actions can cause serious, lasting results, including abuse so destructive that some teenage victims would rather die than continue suffering it. And a social media user's material may prove damaging to the person who posted it, inadvertently harming the person's reputation or job prospects. With so much at risk, some say social media may be best used in a limited fashion, if at all.

Types of Social Media	Purpose	Examples
Blogs, microblogs, podcasts	Messaging and communications	Blogging services: WordPress, Blogger, Tumblr Microblog: Twitter Podcasting services: Jellycast
Services designed to let users upload photos and videos to the Internet	Sharing photos and videos	Photo sharing: Flickr, Instagram Video sharing: YouTube, Vine Photo messaging: Snapchat
Social groups and communities	To network personally or professionally	Facebook, MySpace, LinkedIn
Services that let users bookmark and tag online material with keywords and share links	Social bookmarking and tagging	Delicious, Pinterest
Wikis	Collaboration	Wikipedia
Services that allow users to share their thoughts on goods and services	Providing reviews and opinions	Yelp, Foursquare
Virtual worlds	Real-time interaction with other users via avatars	Second Life, World of Warcraft

PERSONAL RISKS

Social networking encourages people to get to know each other. Facebook and other social networking sites allow users to create profiles with as little or as much information as they want to share. But users can easily share too much or post material that others might find inappropriate or annoying.

A 2014 Pew Research Center poll found that Facebook users disliked several things about the site. The top annoyances were about sharing information. Of those surveyed, 36 percent listed oversharing—people posting too much personal information about themselves—as most annoying. An additional 36 percent noted their top annoyance is when their Facebook friends post information about them without

Oversharing through social media is like telling the world personal secrets.

asking. These are only two of the personal risks of taking part in social media.

Possible Side Effects

What happens online can have effects in the real world. Studies are beginning to find correlations between social media use and real-world problems. Using social media heavily might lead to lower self-control. Studies have also shown a relationship between social media use and overeating when people view images of food. Users may also become more susceptible to peer pressure if they see others "like" something. And researchers at two German universities learned that one-third of Facebook users felt

Social media use can be a problem if a person ignores real-life relationships.

worse—angry, frustrated, or lonely—after visiting the site, often because they compare themselves to other users.

Confirmation bias is another risk. Humans tend to seek information that supports their beliefs rather than information that disproves them. By focusing on information that confirms his or her beliefs, a user might overlook important information or miss learning about or meeting different people. A person who only gets news from one source might not realize other sources are presenting a different take on an issue, for example.

In addition, the information a user consults may be inaccurate. That is because social media has created a world that allows everyone to editorialize or think of

themselves as journalists. Often this citizen journalism reflects confirmation bias, and the information shared might be inaccurate or missing facts that would disprove its argument.

Inappropriate Content

Users can damage their reputations or risk not getting into college or being hired for a job because of the material on their Facebook pages. A 2011 poll of college admissions officers by the education company Kaplan revealed that more than 80 percent of them use Facebook to reach potential students. While snapshots from a party may be fun, they may not reflect well on the person who posts. And a teen user who sexts—sends nude or sexy pictures of himself or herself—can be charged with underage pornography, which is a serious crime.

Some people send explicit images that show pornography, violence, or both. The Internet has a lot of pornography: 30 percent of all data sent across the Internet is related to pornography. Users should avoid downloading images from people they do not know in order to decrease the risk of seeing such photos.

Identity Crisis

Social networking site use may also be causing an identity crisis. Susan Greenfield is a professor at Oxford University

Not Entertained

Psychologist Timothy Wilson studies college students. He has found they struggle within minutes of being without their computer or phone. "One would think we could spend the time mentally entertaining ourselves," Wilson said. "But we can't. We've forgotten how."

who has written about the effects of technology on the brain. She said using Facebook and Twitter has caused millennials to be self-centered, reflecting a childlike desire for constant feedback. Many millennials also have short attention spans. Ultimately, she argues all the time young people spend on social networking sites and playing computer games could change the way they think.

Greenfield shared her views: "What concerns me is the banality of so much that goes out on Twitter. Why should someone be interested in what someone else has had for breakfast? It reminds me of a small child [saying]: 'Look at me ... Look at me. ...' It is almost as if they are in some kind of identity crisis. ... It's almost as if people are living in a world that's not a real world, but a world where what counts is what people think of you or [if they] can click on you."

Liking Is Not Helping

Facebook launched an online culture of liking. With the click of a little graphic showing a thumb pointing up, a user can easily show approval. Other sites, such as YouTube, have adopted the format.

Users also "like" causes, such as humanitarian aid organizations. Liking shows that a user agrees with what the cause is doing. The same is true of posting content about a cause. Blog posts, photographs, videos, and tweets can be great for spreading the word about something. But do not be fooled by that little thumb of approval. The real support is in the giving of time, money, or other resources that will actually help an organization achieve its goals.

The unending flow of information on social media can become overwhelming.

NEGATIVE AND DANGEROUS

Social media can be a breeding ground for negativity. Commenting tools allow users to write whatever they want. Some people write messages intended to annoy or offend other users. The negative posters are known as trolls. The magazine *Popular Science* stopped allowing comments to articles on its website in late 2013. The company made the decision in part because of trolls.

Social media users spread negativity by other channels too. Some apps allow users to anonymously share whatever thoughts or feelings they have without consequence. Because they are not identified, they are not held accountable by friends or family who would

know them if the post were on Facebook. Being unidentifiable can help some people be more open than they normally would.

The anonymity such apps provide has a downside. Like other forms of social media, trolls and bullies can take part. These intentionally hurtful users can spread gossip, negativity, and worse without risk of being identified. Apps that allow such anonymity face a big—if not impossible—task in thwarting abuse.

The anonymity of the Internet can make it hard to stop harassment.

Cyberbullying

Just as people who bully in the real world pick on, taunt, and abuse victims, so do virtual bullies. Cyberbullying is abuse through one or more forms of electronic technology. In addition to hurtful texts or e-mails, cyberbullying includes posts, tweets, photographs, videos, and websites. It also includes making fake online profiles.

Cyberbullying differs from real-world bullying in three distinct ways.

1. It can happen anywhere and at any time.
2. Cyberbullies can post abusive content anonymously, quickly, and to many people at once.
3. Once harmful material has been put online or sent out, removing it is almost impossible.

According to the U.S. Centers for Disease Control's study of youth risk behavior, 14.8 percent of American high school students were cyberbullied in 2013. Bullying affects victims physically and mentally. Kids who are bullied often suffer from depression and anxiety, and they might feel sad and lonely. Victims often have health problems. These

children are more likely than their peers to get lower test scores and grades, miss more school, and even drop out. They might use drugs or alcohol. They may suffer from bullying in the real world too.

Online Predators

Cyberbullies are not the only online threat to children and teens' safety. Online predators hope to connect with potential victims and form relationships. Some online predators want inappropriate photos of young people. Other online predators intend sexual abuse if they can convince their victims to meet them in person.

Predators spend time online in the places teens and children frequent. Social networking sites are particularly appealing because many users post information predators can use to get to know intended victims. Talking about a hobby or interest can make the user think the predator has things in common with him or her. Law enforcement does not know the true prevalence of online predators.

Avoiding Predators

Predators have predictable behavior. First a predator will try to befriend the user. After that the predator will ask for personal information or request pictures. The predator may send photos too, and offer gifts. The predator will talk about sex and may say things that make the intended victim uncomfortable. If a user feels uncomfortable with someone online, he or she should stop communicating and tell his or her parents or guardians what is going on. Not telling could be dangerous.

Criminals

Social media provides a convenient route into people's homes and wallets for criminals. Burglars take advantage of social media by looking for vacation photos. If a user posts photos while on vacation and has not been careful with privacy settings, a thief might be able to identify the house and burglarize it while the user is away.

Some thieves take identities. They can steal a person's identity with only a few pieces of information. Some of that essential data is often available in the user's profile, such as name, date of birth, and city of residence.

Some social media users are deadly. Nona Belomesoff, 18, agreed to meet Christopher James Dannevig in 2010. The Australian teen loved animals and had met Dannevig online. Dannevig had created a fake profile on Facebook stating he worked for a group that helped animals.

Teens Sharing More Private Data

What Teens Post	2006	2012
A photo of themselves	79%	91%
School name	49%	71%
City or town where they live	61%	71%
E-mail address	29%	53%
Cell phone number	2%	20%

The 20-year-old man lured Belomesoff to a meeting by offering her a job. The two would go on a camping trip to look for wounded animals in an area south of Sydney, Australia. Eager to pursue her dream of caring for animals, she agreed. She did not return. Dannevig murdered Belomesoff.

With so many questionable people taking advantage of social media, the utmost care is needed when using it. One option is not using social media at all.

If social media use becomes a problem, one solution is to consider quitting.

EXPLORE THE ALTERNATIVES

Millions and millions of people use social media. Each time they go online to read a blog, update a profile, or check out a favorite celebrity's Twitter feed, users are taking a variety of risks. Instead of surfing social media and networking online, consider the alternatives.

Enjoy Real Life

Almost one-fourth of Americans reported missing out on important events because they were busy on social media trying to share the events, according to a 2012 study by the social networking site Badoo. Instead of sharing the event, take part in it.

Hanging out with friends—without cell phones—is one way to enjoy the real world.

Instead of tweeting a friend, get together. Enjoy real-world time. Hang out. Rather than blog about a favorite thing, do that favorite thing. If a friend has a similar interest, pursue that favorite interest together instead of only in an online community. Communicating in person allows for exchanges that texts and posts do not. People can read one another's expression and hear tones of voice for a deeper understanding of one another.

Enjoying real life also means getting away from the screen and moving. Youth today are less active and more

Reboot asks people each March to take a break from technology for 24 hours as part of the National Day of Unplugging. The national nonprofit encourages people to unplug and "start living a different life: connect with the people in your street, neighborhood and city, have an uninterrupted meal or read a book to your child." Unplugging allows participants to enjoy the real world. Pledges to unplug include reading a book, eating, hugging, dancing, and enjoying nature.

overweight than those of previous generations. One-third of children are overweight, and the rate of childhood obesity has tripled in the last 30 years, according to the Centers for Disease Control. Some parents blame technology, but the adults are at fault as well when 53 percent of them spend free time with their children using a computer or playing video games.

Research shows that children today are not as strong as children were only 10 years ago. Gavin Sandercock, a fitness expert at Essex University in the United Kingdom, compared strength in a group of 315 10-year-olds in 2008 with a group in 1998. The 2008 10-year-olds were weaker.

Playing and exercising outside are important for health.

"This is probably due to changes in activity patterns among English 10-year-olds," he said, "such as taking part in fewer activities like rope-climbing in PE and tree-climbing for fun. Typically, these activities boosted children's strength, making them able to lift and hold their own bodyweight."

Lead author of the study Daniel Cohen said, "Pound for pound, they're weaker and probably carrying more fat."

Try to get your friends off their phones and devices when you're together in real life.

The Parent-Teacher Association (PTA) suggests a variety of activities to get families moving together. They include biking, dancing, gardening, playing a sport, and walking together. Following one or more of the PTA's suggestions will help families get healthier. Doing such activities may just make them happier too.

Proceed with Caution

A computer user may need or want to use social media. School or work may require it. Or the person may simply be interested in taking advantage of some of its possibilities. Whatever the reason, proceed with caution.

The National Cyber Security Alliance lists several tips for staying safe online:

- Use privacy and security settings.
- Remember you cannot take it back.
- Put your best foot forward.
- Be cautious.
- Be aware.
- Be honest with friends about inappropriate material.
- Take action against abuse by blocking the user and reporting him or her to the site.

Social media has so many possibilities—but also so many potential hazards. Fortunately, a user can decide how much to participate and, when taking part, how much to share. Millions of people use social media

Social media should only be used with care, if at all.

without problems. Millions more do not engage in it at all. Understanding its benefits and risks will help users decide if social media is a good fit or if staying away is the thing to do. And when people decide to participate, they will be able to maximize its benefits and limit its risks.

WHAT DO YOU THINK?

- If you use social media, will you change how you use it? How? Why?

- What do you think would make social media most safe to use?

- Have you ever seen or been a victim of cyberbullying? How did it make you feel? What did you do after it happened?

- What do you think about schools using social media? What rules would you suggest for the school and students to follow?

- A person has to be a certain age to do some things, such as 18 years old to vote. Do you think putting an age restriction on social media is a good idea? Would it end some of the problems with social media? Why or why not?

INDEX